Welcome to
SOUTH AUSTRALIA

SOUTH AUSTRALIA

SOUTH AUSTRALIA

THE FRIENDLY STATE

Bunda Cliffs, Great Australian Bight, Nullarbor.

South Australia is known for its stunning landscapes and vibrant culture. From the rolling vineyards of the Barossa Valley where world class wines are crafted, to the rugged beauty of the Flinders Ranges, to breathtaking coastlines, South Australia has it all.

From the capital city of Adelaide with historical architecture to the rich wildlife of Kangaroo Island, this book showcases the hidden gems and natural wonders of South Australia and its diverse landscape.

South Australia, located in the southern central part of Australia, has a

population of 1.8 million people, with most living in the Adelaide area, and Mount Gambier, the second largest population centre.

South Australia is also known for its beautiful nature and wildlife and an array of hundreds of species of birds along with the kangaroos, possums, reptiles and amphibians.

South Australia vastest landscapes with nine deserts including red sand dunes, stony plains and dry salt lakes, as well as some of Australia's most breathtaking beaches and coastlines.

South Australia's state animal, the Southern hairy-nosed wombat (*Lasiorhinus latifrons*).

The 'Piping shrike', or White-backed magpie is South Australia's state bird.

Opal is South Australia's state gemstone.

South Australia's state flower, Sturt's desert pea (*Swainsona formosa*).

Open to all
MARY POPPINS
ADELAIDE CONVENTION CENTRE

ADELAIDE

<— N

Adelaide Botanical Gardens.

Adelaide Railway Station.

Bonython Hall, University of Adelaide.

The Art Gallery of South Australia.

Adelaide city.

Adelaide City Business District.

ADELAIDE CONVENTION CENTRE

Adelaide Museum.

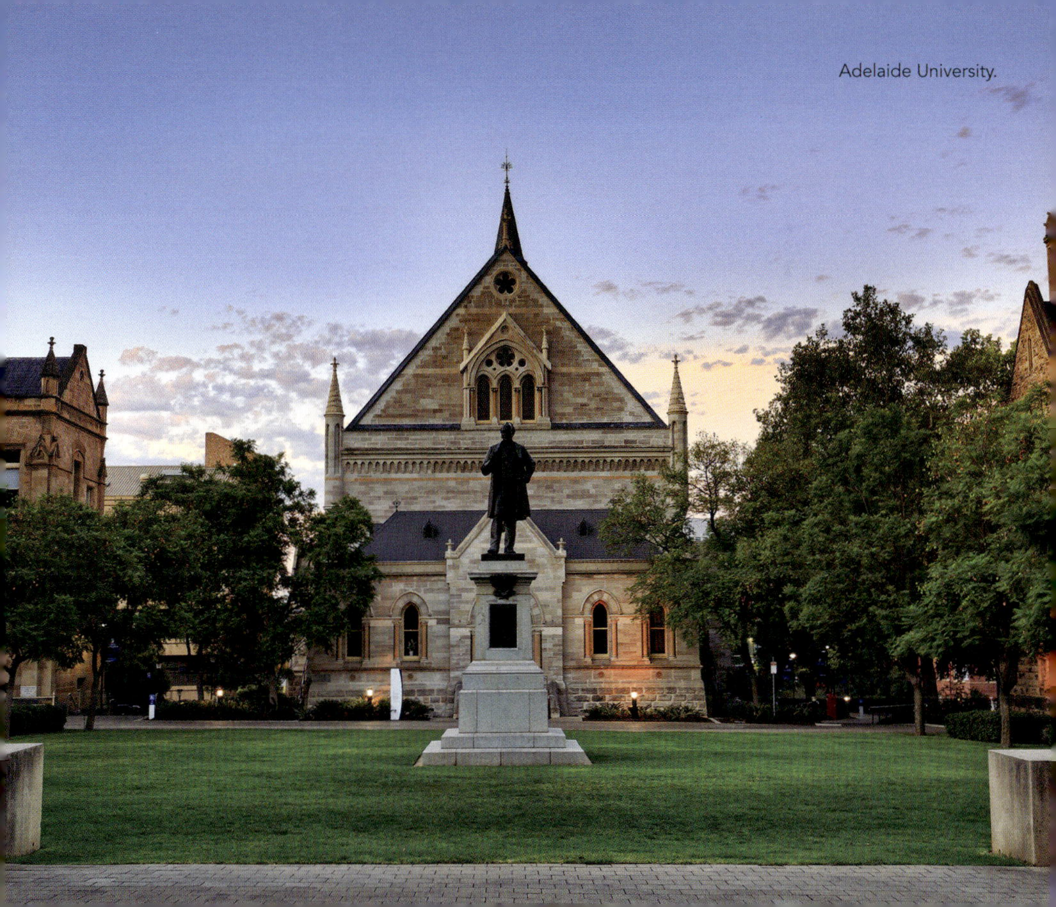

Adelaide University.

Adelaide Botanic Gardens.

Adelaide Botanic Gardens.

St Francis Xavier's Cathedral.

Bradman Collection Museum in Adelaide Oval.

Adelaide city CBD cityscape on shores of Torrens River.

Adelaide Fringe, Australia's biggest arts festival.

Adelaide Fringe.

General Post Office, Adelaide.

Adelaide Entertainment Centre.

Adelaide city view from the hills.

Moseley Square in Glenelg, Adelaide.

Moseley Square Town Hall and Pioneer Monument.

Thebarton Theatre.

University of Adelaide city campus viewed across Goodman Crescent.

Victor Harbour Horse Drawn Tram
on the way to the Granite Island.

Three Rivers Fountain in Victoria Square, Adelaide, designed by John Dowie.

St Peter's Cathedral viewed across Pennington Gardens, Adelaide.

from Adelaide Gaol to Eastern Hills

Adelaide Rotunda in Elder Park,
Adelaide Oval.

Adelaide Symphony Orchestra plays at Symphony Under The Stars at the Adelaide Festival Centre.

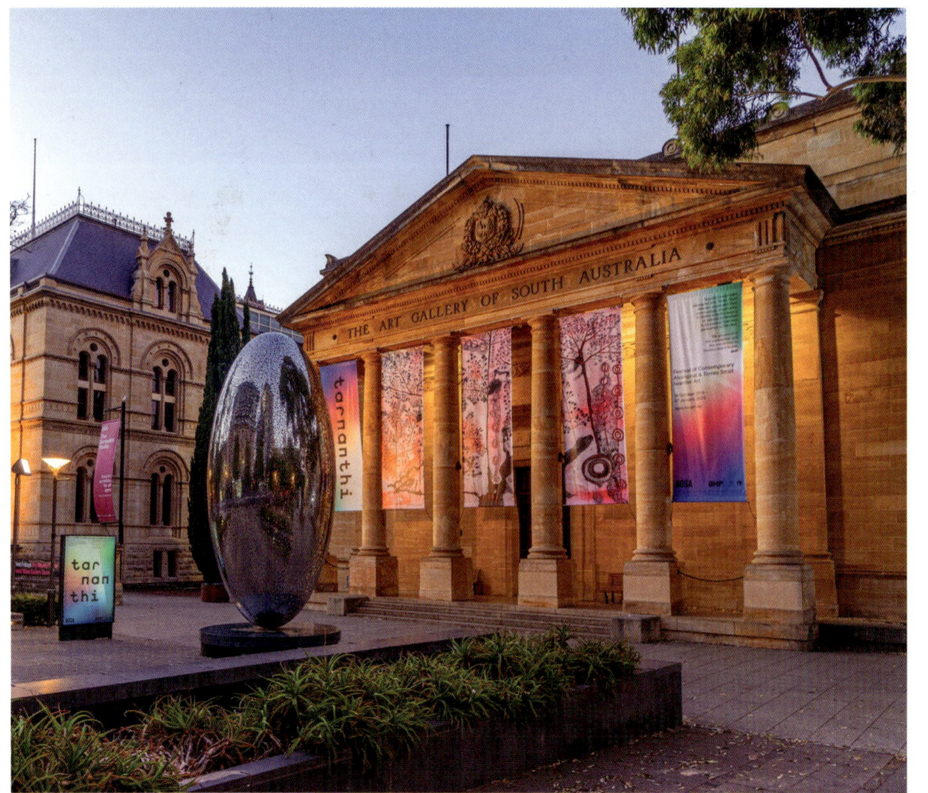

Art Gallery of South Australia.

Beehive Corner.

Adelaide Oval.

South Australian Health and Medical Research Institute (SAHMRI), Adelaide.

Rundle Mall, Adelaide.

St Francis Xavier's Catholic Cathedral.

St Peter's Cathedral.

Flinders University, Adelaide.

Glenelg Beach Skyline Wheel Adelaide.

University of Adelaide campus.

University of South Australia.

Largs Pier Hotel, Largs Bay (near Port Adelaide).

Glenelg Beach jetty.

Brighton Jetty at sunset. Adelaide.

Christies Beach.

Happy Valley Reservoir in Adelaide.

Willunga Beach, Adelaide.

Birkenhead Bridge across Port Adelaide River, Port Adelaide.

Victor Harbour jetty,
Granite Island, Adelaide.

Sunset at the Brighton.

Sunset view of Glenelg Beach Jetty Adelaide.

Vineyards in the Adelaide Hills.

OUTSIDE ADELAIDE

Hahndorf.

Old horse cart in Hahndorf.

Hahndorf, settled by 19th-century Lutheran migrants.

Hahndorf.

McLaren Vale region.

Blackbucks at Monarto Safari Park.

Old Albert Bridge over the River Torrens.

Langmeil Lutheran Churcht, Tanunda.

Black swans on the Murray River.

Mount Lofty, Adelaide Hills.

A kangaroo in the Barossa Valley.

Laratinga Wetlands, Adelaide.

Jacob's Creek vineyard.

Barossa Valley wine region vineyards at sunset time, Tanunda.

An old abandoned house in the Clare Valley.

Clare Valley.

Clare Valley.

Robe.

THE COAST

Robe.

Port Willunga jetty ruins,
Fleurieu Peninsula.

Kangaroos at Deep Creek.

Ferry leaving Kangaroo Island for Cape Jervis.

Remarkable Rocks in Flinders Chase National Park on Kangaroo Island.

Kangaroos at the Remarkable Rocks at Kangaroo Island.

Kangaroos on Kangaroo Island.

Vivonne Bay Rock Pool, Kangaroo Island.

The town of Penneshaw on Kangaroo Island.

Rockpool at Stokes Bay, Kangaroo Island.

Eucalyptus tree tunnel on Kangaroo Island.

Coastline on Kangaroo Island.

Penneshaw, Kangaroo Island.

A pod of inshore bottlenose dolphins swim a wave on the coast of Kangaroo Island.

Flinders Chase National Park, Kangaroo Island.

Flinders Chase National Park, Kangaroo Island.

Hanson Bay on Kangaroo Island.

Admirals Arch in Flinders Chase National Park, Kangaroo Island.

Australian Fur Seal (*Arctocephalus pusillus doriferus*) at Seal Bay Conservation Park, Kangaroo Island.

Cape du Couedic Lighthouse in Flinders Chase National Park on Kangaroo Island.

Kangaroo Island, Pennington Bay.

Kangaroo Island.

Kangaroo on Kangaroo Island.

The Big Lobster is 17 metres high, Kingston SE.

Greenly Beach, Eyre Peninsula.

Hallett Cove Beach.

Jetty on Lake Albert, Meningie.

Brighton Jetty, in Holdfast Bay, Adelaide.

Eyre Penninsula coast.

Eden Valley.

Kangaroo Island ferry terminal in Cape Jervis.

Garden Island Ships' Graveyard.

Maslin Beach with crashing waves at sunset, Fleurieu Peninsula.

Majestic vista of inside Wilpena Pound rock formation in Flinders Ranges.

Wilpena Pound is an eroded mountain range.

Wilpena Pound.

Murray Mouth, Coorong.

Ceduna Thevenard Port.

Flinders Ranges in the vicinity of the village of Blinman.

Murray River.

Old winery buildings in the Clare Valley.

Rapid Bay.

Pichi Richi tourist steam train ride in Flinders Ranges.

Quorn, final stop for the Pichi Richi railway.

Onkaparinga River mouth in South Port, Port Noarlunga.

Port Noarlunga shared footpath and bike track along the Onkaparinga River.

Salt Creek, Coorong.

Cazneaux tree, Flinders Ranges.

Second Valley beach with jetty at sunset, Fleurieu Peninsula.

O'Sullivan Beach.

O'Sullivan Beach bicycle track.

South Port beach stairs viewed towards Onkaparinga River.

Stokes Bay Beach, Kangaroo Island.

RAILWAY CROSSING
STOP
LOOK FOR TRAINS
RAILWAY

CROSSING

Sunset at Sellicks Beach.

The Blue Lake, a large crater lake located in a dormant volcanic maar near Mount Gambier in the Limestone Coast.

The Blue Lake.

The d'Arenberg Cube among Mourvèdre vines, McLaren Vale.

The Murray Mouth, Coorong.

The Doorway Rock in Robe, Cape Dombey, Limestone Coast.

The Granites, Coorong.

View of salt lake at Coorong National Park. The pink coloration caused by algae called *Dunaliella salina*.

Australian pelicans (*Pelecanus conspicillatus*), Coorong.

Australian pelicans, Coorong.

Coorong National Park.

Salt Lake on the Eyre Peninsula off the Flinders Highway in Wudinna.

Sand dunes in Coorong National Park.

280 million years old archaeological site of Hallett Cove Sugarloaf.

Wilpena Pound historic Hills homestead at the gap in Flinders Ranges.

WIlpena Pound rock formation peaks at sunset in Flinders Ranges.

Emu family at Port Lincoln National Park.

Wreck of the *Pisces Star* at Cape Banks.

Bunda Cliffs, Great Australian Bight, Nullarbor.

Cape Spencer Lighthouse, Yorke Peninsula.

Centenary Tower, views of Mount Gambier.

Little Blue Lake, Mount Gambier.

Mount Gambier Cave Garden

Umpherston Sinkhole Cave Gardens, Mt Gambier, Limestone Coast.

Umpherston Sinkhole, Mount Gambier.

Umpherston Sinkhole Cave Gardens, Mt Gambier.

Coffin Bay National Park, Eyre Peninsula.

Coffin Bay on the Eyre Peninsula.

Eyre Peninsula.

Flinders Ranges.

hill on the horizon near Port Augusta.

Ikara-Flinders Ranges National Park.

Monarto Safari Park.

Paringa bridge over the Murray River.

Murphy's Haystacks, Mortana, between Streaky Bay and Port Kenny on the Eyre Peninsula.

Oyster farm in Coffin Bay, Eyre Peninsula

Pildappa Rock, Eyre Peninsula.

Lake MacDonnell on the Eyre Peninsula outside of Point Sinclair in Penong.

South Australian vineyard.

Stuart Highway a side road takes you to Kingoonya and Tarcoola via a dirt track which is seasonally closed or continue along the highway to Pimba and Port Augusta.

Tcharkuldu rock granite formations, Gawler Ranges National Park, Eyre Peninsula.

Tantanoolas Cave,
Mount Gambier.

Tantanoolas Cave,
Mount Gambier.

Limestone cave at Naracoorte Caves National Park.

Victoria Fossil Cave, Naracoorte Caves.

Naracoorte Caves.

The Ghan train departing Adelaide Parklands Terminal on its way to Darwin.

The Bend Motorsport Park.

Whyalla.

Whyalla Wetlands.

The Painted Desert, 120 kilometres north-east of Coober Pedy.

OUTBACK

Hawker, gateway to Flinders Ranges.

Andamooka opal fields.

Ghan train line crossing the Stuart Highway.

Andamooka.

Andamooka, mining town.

Historical mine workers cottage in opal mining town Andamooka.

Andamooka Opal Hotel.

Coober Pedy Opal Fields Golf Course.

Serbian Orthodox underground Church of Saint Elijah the Prophet in Coober Pedy.

UNDERGROUND
SERBIAN
ORTHODOX CHURCH
SAINT ELIJAH

First published in 2025 by New Holland Publishers

newhollandpublishers.com

A record of this book is held at the National Library of Australia.

ISBN 9781760792046

Managing Director: Fiona Schultz
General Manager/Publisher: Olga Dementiev
Designer: Andrew Davies
Production Director: Arlene Gippert

Keep up with New Holland Publishers:

NewHollandPublishers

@newhollandpublishers